D0557670

Roses
forNorthernGardeners

By David Harrap

Homeworld

The Publisher:

Lone Pine Publishing   **Lone Pine Publishing**
#206, 10426-81 Avenue   #202A 1110 Seymour Street
Edmonton, Alberta, Canada   Vancouver, B.C., Canada
T6E 1X5   V6B 3N3

Canadian Cataloguing in Publication Data
Harrap, David, 1945-
        Roses for Northern Gardeners

        (Homeworld)
        ISBN 1-55105-031-5
        1. Rose culture — Canada. I. Title. II. Series.
SB411.5.C3H37 1993   635.9'33372'0971 c93-091453-8

Editor-in-chief: *Glenn Rollans*
Editorial: *Debby Shoctor*
Cover and original illustrations: *Linda Dunn*
Design, layout and cover: *Carol McKellar*
Printing: *Friesen Printers, Altona, Manitoba, Canada.*

The publisher gratefully acknowledges the assistance of the Department of
Canadian Heritage and Alberta Community Development and the financial
support provided by the Alberta Foundation for the Arts in the production of
this book.

Contents

A Rose is a Rose

HISTORY RECORDS THAT THE ROSE has been grown and loved for thousands of years. It has been the official emblem of nations. Soldiers have marched into battle wearing the rose. Its fragrance is legendary: the Romans, it is said, would give an adversary a rose to smell to cool his anger.

Few flowers are so steeped in history. This was the favourite flower of the Romans, who spread its culture wherever their armies conquered. From the gardens of Chinese emperors to the beautiful garden at Malmaison tended by the Empress Josephine, wife of Napoleon, the rose has had pride of place. And the love affair continues on down to our day as the rose is still the world's most popular flower.

In its wild state, the rose is found only in the Northern Hemisphere. There are at least 150 recognized species (true Wild roses) and literally thousands of cultivated varieties.

It is one of the most versatile garden plants and can be grown for its attractive hips, leaves, canes and thorns, as well as for its beautiful flowers and fragrance. Many varieties produce a succession of flowers throughout the whole summer, and colours are endless: from the purest white, through yellow, orange and pink, to the deepest velvety crimson. As a garden plant the rose is unsurpassed.

Classification of roses

For the sake of simplicity, roses can be divided into the following broad groups:

- Species or Wild roses;

- Old Garden roses — includes Gallica, Damask, Alba and Centifolia;

- Modern roses — includes Hybrid Tea, Floribunda, Grandiflora, Shrub and Miniatures.

In addition, there are Climbing and Rambler roses, Tree (Standard) roses, patio and ground-cover roses.

Our northern climate adds a challenge to our rose growing endeavours, but we can grow most types of roses, being limited only by the extent of our own ingenuity, or the efforts we are willing to put forth. Whenever you state categorically that "you can't grow those roses here," you quickly discover that there are lots of gardeners who do, and very successfully, I might add.

As a group, the hardiest types are the Species or Wild roses. Some of these will survive -40° C, even without protection (see list), but the vast majority of roses are classified as "tender" and therefore require some type of protection over the winter. Most of the Old Garden roses bloom on second-year wood (canes produced the previous season), so they are not recommended for cold winter areas of the country. (Winter kill cuts these types of canes back too much.) The same problem applies to Rambler and many of the Climbing roses — particularly the older varieties.

As the vast majority of Modern roses bloom on canes that are produced the same season, these are generally the types we grow in our northern gardens. Except for the odd exception, Modern roses are still considered tender and will need winter protection, but as these types send up flowering canes from the base of the bush, all is not lost when winter cuts back a good percentage of the canes.

Bad locations for roses include:

- under the drip line of trees;
- within 45 cm of house walls and foundations;
- in badly-drained ground;
- areas where they only receive full sun just a few hours a day.

Preparing the flower beds

While it might be true that there are only a few places on this earth where roses won't grow, attention should still be given to ensure that the selected site is the very best available. Roses need a sunny position. They will tolerate a little shade during part of the day, but the less the better. Morning sun is very important as it allows the plants to dry off quickly after early morning dew, thus reducing the problems from fungal diseases that occur under moist conditions.

If roses are grown in very shady locations, they will be spindly, produce few if any flowers, and be prone to a great many insects and diseases.

Roses like an open but sheltered position, with good air circulation. They do not like windy, exposed sites. Also, they do not like to compete with other plants for nutrients, moisture and light. For this reason, give them lots of room.

Soil preparation

Roses adapt to many types of soil but they do have one fundamental requirement: moisture. The soil must provide adequate moisture at all times, along with good drainage so water does not collect around the roots. Roses (like most plants) dislike "wet feet." A rich, loamy soil is the ideal.

Soil should be deeply dug, incorporating plenty of organic material such as well-rotted farmyard manure, garden compost, peat moss (wet it first), spent mushroom compost, or shredded pine bark. Heavy soil can be improved with these soil amendments.

A soil pH slightly on the acid side — between 6.0 and 6.5 — is what roses prefer. Rose beds should always be prepared well in advance of planting as the soil must be allowed to settle. Ideally, beds should be dug in the fall in preparation for spring planting.

How to select healthy plants

Rose bushes are sold in three different ways:

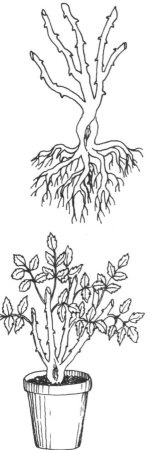

• Bare-root bushes available by mail order from rose nurseries. These are plants that are lifted at the nursery and have the soil removed from around the roots before plants are shipped. They are usually sent with the bare roots wrapped in plastic, newspaper or wood wool.

• Packaged bare-root bushes sold in stores. This type of plant usually has peat moss, wood chips or shredded paper around the roots and is in a plastic or waxed cardboard container. No matter what it might say on the package, this is still a bare-root rose and should be treated as such. With this method of packaging, the canes are dipped in wax.

• Container-grown plants that are sometimes in bloom when you buy them.

Commercially, rose bushes are graded into different sizes, just like eggs, vegetables and fruit. In North America there are three grades:

1) Bushes that have three or more strong, thick canes. Two of the canes being at least 45 cm (18") long.

1.5) Bushes that have two canes at least 38 cm (15") long. (Sometimes this grade may be called 1A.)

2) Bushes that have two canes 30 cm (12") long.

Usually these grades apply to the Shrub, Hybrid Tea, Floribunda and other large bush varieties.

Terminology

Many roses in the stores are sold as "Two-year-old Field Grown," but this doesn't really tell you much, as most bushes take about two years before they can be marketed, and, invariably, roses are grown in a field! On some packaged roses the term "Jumbo" is used. This is an ambiguous trade classification, however, referring to size, but it does not necessarily have reference to quality as the various parts of a rose bush must be in proportion to one another. A rose bush with exceptionally thick and heavy canes is of little worth if the roots resemble stubby, chopped-off fingers. If a rose bush will not grow — and a good root system is imperative for the establishment of a newly planted bush — then it is never a bargain, no matter what the price or description on the package.

What to look for

- **Look at the canes.** These should be green, firm, plump, never shrivelled. (If they are shrivelled, this could indicate that the bushes are dehydrated due to improper storage.) Any visible pith should be white or green, not tan or brown, as this could indicate frost damage or disease. No matter what grade, the canes on the enlarged-flowered bushes should be at least pencil thick.

A Rose is a Rose

- **Look at the rootstock neck.** This is the stem between the roots and the bud union (the knobby area from where the canes originate). It should be of thumb thickness. Necks that are thin and spindly indicate a poor quality plant. Some packaged plants have very long necks — over 8 cm (3"). (It's almost as though they are custom-grown solely to fit the package.) While these plants are all right, they are a little more awkward to plant.

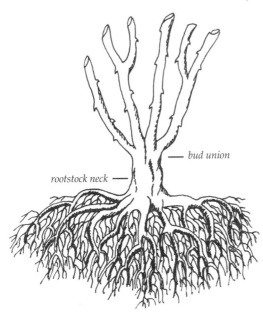

bud union

rootstock neck

- **Look at the roots.** Not too easy with packaged plants, but maybe you can sneak a peek! There should be an excellent root system with plenty of long, fibrous roots. Plants that have a good many of their roots chopped off, or ones that have only a couple of pathetic-looking roots, are a poor buy. It cannot be over-emphasized how important a viable root system is to the plant, and yet, with many gardeners, roots are often the last thing they think about.

- **Look at the shoots.** Ideally, there should not be any, as bare-root roses are sold in a dormant state. In practice, however, it usually doesn't work this way. After the plant leaves the grower it is often subjected to unsuitable temperatures that cause the buds to break dormancy and start growing shoots. Then what? If shoot growth is only minimal, the plant should come to no harm, providing it is planted correctly. If the shoots are about 5 cm (2") or more in length they should be removed, as chances are they will wither and die anyway. The dormant, auxiliary bud-eyes will then become activated and replace any growth that was removed. It's also a good idea to inspect the bud-eyes carefully to see if they have been damaged or rubbed off.

Packaged roses should be purchased as soon as they become available in the stores; even if you can't plant them immediately, at least you will be able to control the storage conditions somewhat. Many of the packaged roses have their canes dipped in wax. This is to prevent dehydration and subsequent damage to the bush. Waxing thus gives the plant a longer shelf life, and also aids against dehydration at planting time.

Buying container-grown roses

These should be plants that have been growing for several months in containers and not recently potted-up bare-root bushes. Things to look for:

- Mossy, green growth on top of the soil — indicates rose has not been recently transplanted;

- Roots starting to grow through the drainage holes;

- Plant does not pull straight out of the soil when lifted by the canes;

- Containers that are suitable for the size of the plant — at least 9 L (2 gal.). Containers for Miniature roses would be much smaller, of course;

- No die-back of the canes — this might be a sign that the plant has been far too long in the container.

Caring for your roses prior to planting

Bare-root bushes

Plants received through the mail should be unpacked carefully and examined. **Never expose the roots to the elements at any time**, as once roots dry out, the plant cannot be saved. If the bushes are in good condition — canes plump and firm, roots nice and moist — they can be returned to the original packing and stored in a cool, frost-free place until planting time. Plants can be safely stored like this for a week to ten days.

If you receive the plants in poor condition, maybe due to lengthy shipping, and canes are shrivelled and dry, then soak the whole plant (canes as well as roots) overnight in cold water. Again, if the weather does not allow you to plant immediately, they should be stored using the following method, as the original packaging may be of no further use:

- Spread a sheet of plastic on the floor, then add a couple of layers of dry newspapers. Put the roses in a pile on top, and completely cover with very moist peat or sawdust, making sure it filters down all around the canes and roots. Cover the whole pile with wet burlap sacks and finally a loosely fitting piece of plastic. Providing the temperature can be kept cool and frost-free, roses can be stored this way for up to three or four weeks. If you notice the sacks and peat starting to dry out, then wet the whole pile down.

Boxed and packaged roses are only available in the spring, so they can usually be planted right away. However, if you are unable to plant immediately, store them in a cool frost-free place. **Never store roses in a warm house.**

How to Plant Roses

I N COLD-WINTER AREAS OF THE country where temperatures drop below -25° C (-10° F), the best time to plant dormant bushes is in the spring: April to early May at the latest. Try to plant roses as soon as the frost is out of the ground and it can be safely worked. It's important for the plants to establish themselves before hot, dry weather arrives.

Planting

Remove roses from their packing or storage. Trim off broken or damaged roots, then immerse the whole bush in a large pail of cold water. Do not let the bushes lie around with their roots exposed even for a few minutes. Some rosarians soak their bushes overnight, some use muddy water. As long as the plants are in good condition, I find half an hour is plenty.

Dig a hole that will be large enough to accommodate all the roots comfortably so none are cramped; it's important to spread out the roots as much as possible.

Do not dig an excessively deep hole thinking that the roots go straight down — they don't. It is much better to position the plant in such a way that some of the roots sit flat on the bottom of the hole. The exact depth of the bud union (the knobby lump from where the canes originate) will depend on the severity of the winter climate in your area.

Many roses have their roots running in one direction rather than all around. These bushes should be planted to one side of the hole so roots are not cramped.

Mix a little peat moss and bone meal into the excavated soil and use this to backfill the hole. Before putting the bush in the hole, add a shovelful of soil to the bottom. Position the bush in the hole and spread the roots out in a fan-shape.

Holding the top of the canes with one hand, sprinkle the soil mixture over the roots using your other hand. Shake the canes as you backfill the hole to ensure soil filters down all around the roots. When the hole is half-filled, firm the soil by treading. Continue filling the hole to soil level. Firm again, and add more soil if needed. Leave a slight depression around the bush for watering.

Firm planting is very important as all the roots must be making good contact with the soil. Many failures at planting time are caused by loose soil around the roots; in effect, the roots dry out because they have no contact with soil particles. (When firming the soil, do not compact it to such an extent that you damage the soil structure. This is the reason you should never work in the garden if the ground is soggy or waterlogged.)

Give each bush a good watering, being careful not to wash away soil from around the plants.

Depth of bud union

The bud union is a vital part of the rose and must be adequately protected in winter if the plant is to survive — winter protection of your roses begins at planting time.

In areas that experience minimum winter temperatures of -23° C (-8° F), the bud union should be 5–8 cm (2–3″) below soil level. In extremely cold areas of the country, with minimum winter temperatures of -29° C (-15° F) and lower, the bud union should be 8–10 cm (3–4") below soil level.

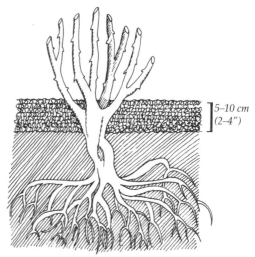

5–10 cm
(2–4")

Bushes with long necks might have to be planted at a slant so the roots are not forced too deep, especially if the bud union must be 8–10 cm (3–4") below ground.

Some gardeners mix in perlite or fine granite grit to the soil that directly covers the bud union. This will lighten up the soil making it easier for the basal shoots to break through the ground. Also, during the growing season it's a good idea to scoop out a shallow depression at the base of the bush so the bud union is not too deep.

Planting distances

Climate, site, and type of cultivar will all have a bearing on planting distances. Also, many gardeners are getting away from the old habit of planting the roses in one bed altogether; they spot them here and there, with other garden plants.

As a general guide, Hybrid Tea, Floribunda and Grandiflora roses can be planted from 45–90 cm (18–36") apart; Shrub roses 90–120 cm (36–48") apart; the Species roses require a lot more room.

In mild climates roses should be planted further apart, as winterkill is not so severe and the bushes, therefore, make more substantial growth.

Also, be familiar with the growth habits of the varieties you buy; notice, too, how similar plants grow in local gardens. That should give you an idea on planting distances.

Pruning newly planted roses

First, remove damaged or broken canes, then cut each cane back to an outward-growing bud 20–25 cm (8–10″) above the ground. Vigorous Shrub and Species roses are not cut back so hard.

A general rule to follow when pruning is: **cut back weak, spindly growth harder than thicker canes.**

Many gardeners cannot bring themselves to cut back their nice new plants so drastically, but it really is necessary if you want your roses to do well after transplanting. Remember, the rose bush you buy has been trimmed by the grower, but now the gardener needs to prune it.

Protecting the canes after planting

A major cause of plants dying or failing to grow vigorously after planting is dehydration. It takes about three weeks for the plant to make new feeder roots, so during that time when the root system is unable to supply any water, the canes must be protected from drying out.

The easiest method is to mound up the canes with soil. If the

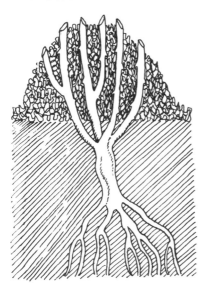

plants have been pruned as recommended, then most of the canes will be covered by the mound. In about three weeks, new growth should start to appear. Gradually remove the soil a bit at a time, thus allowing the new tender shoots to harden off. If hard frosts threaten, carefully replace the soil mound.

Occasionally, a bush will refuse to break dormancy. Try mounding the plant with moist peat and cover the mound with a plastic bag.

Protecting Tree roses

Even in a cold climate a few gardeners try their hand at growing Tree, or Standard, roses. They are available by mail order in the spring, usually bare-rooted.

After planting, put moist wood wool over the canes, then cover with a brown paper bag. Cut a couple of holes in the corner of the bag and leave over the head of the Tree rose until the buds break dormancy, which should be within three weeks. Give the wood wool an occasional spraying to keep it moist.

Planting Climbing and Rambler roses

Again, some like to grow these type of roses. Unfortunately, most of the Rambler roses and the older Climbing roses flower on canes produced the previous season. As most of this wood is winter-killed, all you end up with every year (providing, of course, the rootstock survives the winter) are flowerless basal shoots.

If you are intent on growing these roses (some gardeners go to the extent of taking down all the canes off their supports and burying them in a trench over the winter) plant them in the same manner as outlined above.

A note about labels

Wire tags should not be left on the plants as they will cut into the stems as the bushes grow, thereby providing a possible entry site for disease.

Planting container-grown plants

Dig a hole as you would for a bare-root rose, then place some of the planting mixture in the bottom of the hole. Remove the plant from the container and break up the rootball a little. Try to spread out the roots somewhat, as often the roots will tend to stay massed together even after transplanting; this is especially important if the plant has been too long in the container and is now pot-bound. Fill up the hole in the usual manner. Container-grown roses are planted at the same depth as bare-root plants.

Containers should be well-watered the day before planting as you should never set out a dry plant.

While you should not have to mound up container-grown roses after planting (providing they are *growing*, with leaves and shoots) it will still need protecting from the hot sun just like any other plant after transplanting. Do your planting during cool, cloudy weather, and shade the plants from the sun for a few days.

Remember that a container-grown plant is not considered to be successfully transplanted until it has grown into the surrounding soil.

Moving established plants

Loosen the plant all the way around, then dig deeper to locate and lift out the main roots; long roots can be chopped off to facilitate lifting. It is not necessary to keep any soil around the roots when lifting. Once the plant is dug up, handle the bush as a bare-root plant. Trim off broken or damaged roots and remove suckers and any old, dead stumps.

Replant very firmly and keep well-watered. Provide the necessary protection from the elements as you would for a new plant.

Sometimes moving old plants can give them a new lease on life. So if your old rose bushes are not growing too well, try moving them. But if the old bush is over the hill, give it a decent burial and plant a new one! Don't waste time and effort growing sick plants.

In our climate, the time to move bushes is early spring, as soon as the ground can be worked and while the plants are still dormant.

Reasons why roses grow poorly or not at all

1) Poor quality plant to begin with.

2) Desiccated plant due to improper storage at nursery. (Nurseries dig up plants in late fall and keep them in storage over the winter.)

3) Plant D.O.A. (dead on arrival — roots frosted in transit).

4) Roots dried out before planting.

5) Loose planting — soil not firmed.

6) Plant desiccated because not mounded.

7) Not pruned back after planting so too many canes with too many shoots; as a result plant desiccated before root system became established.

8) Soil dried out.

Caring for Roses
During the Growing Season

Cultivation

WHEN CULTIVATING THE SOIL AROUND roses, do not dig too deeply, as you can damage near-surface roots. A light hoeing around the bushes to keep weeds to a minimum should suffice. Every spring and fall incorporate well-rotted garden compost and a little bone meal in to the top 3–5 cm (1–2″) of soil.

Watering

Roses need lots of moisture in the soil to perform well. The amount of watering necessary will depend on the climate and type of soil — whether heavy or sandy loam. Providing there is good drainage, it is very hard to overwater roses.

Lack of water will cause stress to the plants: they will make little new growth and the bushes become susceptible to pests and diseases.

To facilitate watering, make a shallow depression around each bush, being careful not to damage any roots. Soaker hoses or slow-drip irrigation systems are ideal as the water is applied slowly and does not run off.

When it comes to watering, it's not so much a case of how much water you put on the flower beds, but **how deeply the water is penetrating.**

The soil must be moist around the root zone, which means the water should soak down to a depth of at least 30 cm (12"). Just because there is a heavy rainfall does not necessarily mean the roots receive sufficient moisture — perhaps most of it ran off.

In mid-summer, each plant might need the equivalent of 20 L (5 gal.) per week and sometimes a lot more, especially if the weather is hot and dry. Light and frequent sprinklings are not recommended as they encourage a shallow root system that will not adequately support the plants.

Hot weather watering

During hot weather a plant may transpire up to 99% of the water that is taken up by the roots. This will cause wilting or flagging, and if allowed to continue without replacing the moisture in the soil, the plant will die. This gives you some idea of how important good water management is for the health of your roses.

Feeding

Too many chemical fertilizers are already used on the land, and that includes our gardens. Most of the chemical fertilizers we use are leached out of reach of plant roots, so in effect, we are often just wasting our money and hurting the environment when we pour all these fertilizers on the garden.

Roses certainly need a rich, fertile soil, and herein lies the clue to successful soil management: **feed the soil, not the plants.** And the best way to feed soil is to dig in organic matter such as well-rotted manure and garden compost. It's the soil that makes everything possible, and when you take care of this precious medium for growth, you will have healthy plants.

From time to time you could consider using the following **rose tonics**, but not to replace the soil amendments already mentioned:

Epsom salts (magnesium sulphate)

A good source of magnesium (essential for the formation of chlorophyll). Epsom salts can encourage the production of basal breaks, improve production of blossoms, and add to the overall health of your roses. Give each bush 28 g (1 oz.) in spring and again in midsummer. (When the plants are in full leaf it is best applied as a foliar feed.)

Gypsum (calcium sulphate)

Very useful in helping to flush from the soil harmful salts that might have accumulated due to heavy fertilizer use. Good for container plants as it conditions the soil against compaction, thereby increasing permeability. Also used in soil preparation when ground is heavy and alkaline. Apply 60 g (2 oz.) to each bush in early spring, and carefully work it into the top 5 cm (2") of soil. Water it in. Container plants should receive 30 g (1 oz.) As gypsum will not increase the alkalinity; it will **not** neutralize soil acidity.

Fish emulsion

An excellent tonic that can stimulate budding and blooming of roses, as well as greening-up the foliage. Can be used throughout the season as a liquid feed. Fish emulsion can be applied over mulches. (Fish meal is a dry form that can be lightly forked in around bushes in spring, or whenever beds are lightly hoed.)

Mulching

Mulching your rose beds can be quite beneficial in a number of ways:

- Slows down evaporation from the soil, thus conserving moisture.

- Prevents crusting and compaction of soil.

- Helps control weed growth.

- Keeps soil and roots cooler in summer.

- Protects surface roots that could be damaged by cultivation.

- Prevents soil from spattering lower leaves.

- Supplies organic matter to the soil when dug in.

- Pleasing to the eye if attractive mulches are used.

Once the soil warms up in the spring, spread an 8-cm (3") layer of mulch over the rose beds. Shredded leaves, spent mushroom compost or bark can be used. Unless peat moss is kept permanently damp, it is not recommended, as it has the habit of shedding water when it becomes dry. Also avoid using materials that have a tendency to crust over, as they too will cause water to run off.

Mulches can use up soil nitrogen as they decompose, so it's best to use materials that are already well composted. Because of this, sawdust is not recommended.

Keep the mulch a few centimetres from the base of the bushes.

Disbudding

If you are growing roses for exhibition, then it will be necessary to disbud the large-flowered varieties, particularly Hybrid Teas and Floribundas. Disbudding restricts the number of blooms on a stem, thus increasing the size of the remaining flowers.

The purpose of disbudding is to direct the maximum amount of energy to a remaining bud or buds. To be effective, therefore, this operation must be carried out while the buds are still very small, and not just before blooming.

The easiest way to disbud a rose is to pinch out the bud using your finger and thumb.

Dead-heading

This is a term used to describe the removing of faded flower heads from rose bushes. The purpose of dead-heading is to accelerate the production of the next crop of blooms. Only

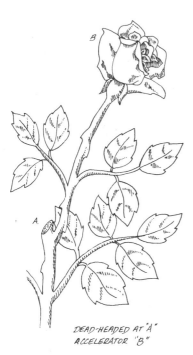

varieties that are repeat-flowering should be dead-headed. Many of the Shrub and Species roses produce very attractive hips in the fall and should not be dead-headed.

Using a sharp pair of pruners, remove the faded bloom and a little of the stem down to just above the first healthy leaf-axil bud. (For the correct way to prune a rose cane, see "Pruning," p. 33.)

Remember, however, that roses need leaves — these are the "food factories" — so when dead-heading, remove as little foliage as possible. This is especially important with first-year bushes.

DEAD-HEADED AT "A"
ACCELERATOR "B"

Suckers

Many of the bushes you buy are actually a combination of two types of roses: the rootstock (usually a Species or Wild rose), and the selected cultivated variety that is budded onto the rootstock. This will often produce a more vigorous plant than one grown on its own roots. This is particularly the case when the cultivated variety has been bred for merits other than the strength of its root system. Wild roses are renowned for their vigorous root systems.

By definition, a sucker is an unwanted shoot from the rootstock. They **always** originate from **below** the bud union.

It's important to remove suckers as soon as possible, for if allowed to remain, they will eventually outgrow and smother the plant.

Many books tell you that suckers have lighter-green leaves with seven leaflets, and thorns of a different shape and colour. This is not a reliable way to identify a sucker. Many roses, particularly Species, Shrub, Climbers and Ramblers have leaflets similar to the rootstock. The best way to identify a sucker is to look at the **point of origin**. If you suspect one, carefully scrape away some of the soil from around the shoot and see where it originates. If it comes from below the bud union, then you've found a sucker. (With experience you will readily recognize a sucker without having to dig around the bush — the shoot in question will just not look *right*.)

Remove the sucker by pulling it off as close as possible to its point of origin on the rootstock. Do not simply cut it off at ground level; this "pruning" will stimulate the development of dormant buds on the rootstock and the sucker will be back twice as vigorous.

If the sucker is too large for pulling without loosening the plant, cut it off flush with the root, or even remove the whole root if it's more practical.

Caring for Roses During the Growing Season

Tree roses are prone to sucker, especially on the stem. These suckers should be rubbed off while still small. If they are a little too long, cut them off cleanly, flush with the stem. Do not damage the bark.

Growing Roses in Containers

R OSES LEND THEMSELVES TO CONTAINER gardening. Basically, if you can grow a rose in the ground, you can grow it in a pot.

Reasons for growing roses in containers:

- Movable plants that can be located in the "ideal spot", especially if lack of sun is a problem;

- allows tender varieties to be grown as containers can be buried in the winter (for how to do this, see pp. 43–45);

- adds interest to paved areas;

- brings the roses closer to outdoor-sitting areas so you can enjoy their fragrance and form.

Containers should be large enough for the particular variety, and able to hold a sufficient amount of soil so they are not constantly drying out.

For most roses, choose containers that are at least 35–45 cm (14–18") wide and 45–50 cm (18–20") deep. If the plants are to stay in the pots for only one growing season, then slightly smaller containers can be used — such as a 23 L (5 gal.) size. Miniatures can be grown in 15–20 cm (6-8") pots.

Wooden tubs and planters make ideal containers as they generally keep the soil temperature cooler than if using plastic. Unglazed clay pots can dry out very quickly if not carefully watched during periods of warm weather. Metal containers are not recommended as they conduct cold and heat too quickly. Any container used should be sturdy yet light enough to be moved.

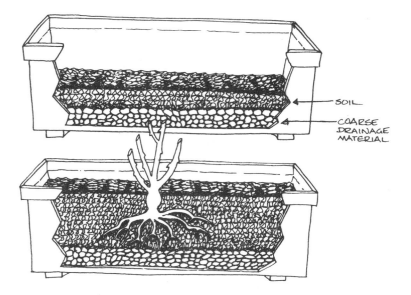

SOIL

COARSE DRAINAGE MATERIAL

All containers must have plenty of drainage holes in the bottom so water can drain freely.

Rather than using straight soil in your containers, use a mixture of three parts sandy loam, two parts well-rotted garden compost (must be **well-rotted**) and one part horticultural sand or sharp granite grit.

If necessary, roots can be trimmed to fit the containers; this is preferable to bunching up the roots, or folding them double.

Centre the rose (if the roots allow), spread the roots out, then fill up the container with the soil mix. As you go, slap the sides of the container with your hands to help filter down the soil around the roots; it's very important there be no air pockets.

Be sure to leave at least 5 cm (2") of space between soil level and the tops of the containers for watering. If you intend to use a mulch, then a little more space must be left. Finally, water the container until you notice water seeping out of the drainage holes. As with all watering, never direct a heavy jet of water, as this will punch holes in the soil, exposing the roots.

Warning!

Dark-coloured plastic pots and similar containers absorb a lot of heat, so the sides must be shaded from direct sun during hot weather. If the soil becomes too hot — over 40° C (104° F) — the root system can be killed.

Watering

When watering containers, do it thoroughly and deeply. Enough water should be applied so it reaches down through the root zone and starts to run out of the drainage holes. This illustrates the importance of providing good drainage within the containers, for without it, the soil can become a soggy mess and consequently harm the plants.

If the weather is extremely wet for any length of time — particularly after planting — cover the surface of the containers to prevent water-logging.

Warning signs

Signs of water shortage: container feels light when lifted; clay pots "ring" when tapped with a piece of wood; leaves start to droop; foliage has a dull, parched look; no new growth; flower stems wilt and hang down; dead plant!

Signs of overwatering: A saturated soil that drips water when squeezed — even quite a while after watering; leaves turn yellow at the base of the plant, fall off; stunted growth. Even more serious is what is happening within the container: roots cease to function properly; development of root-rotting organisms; root system dies.

Feeding

Because of the frequent need to water containers, nutrients are leached (washed) from the soil through the drainage holes. Because of this it becomes necessary from time to time to replace lost nutrients. (A sign that nutrients are being leached from containers is a powdery deposit around drainage holes.)

An ideal feeding program for container plants is to incorporate a slow-release fertilizer into the soil mixture at planting time, and supplement this with a few applications of fish emulsion. (Slow-release fertilizers supply nutrients over an extended period of time, unlike quick-acting fertilizers that "deliver the goods" all at once.)

Cutting Flowers
for the House

ROSES SHOULD BE ENJOYED INSIDE the house as well as out in the garden.

Five steps for lasting cut flowers:

1) Cut flowers when the temperature is cool — **never** during the heat of the day, or when hot sun is on the bushes. Early morning or evening is best.

2) Fill up a clean bucket with warm water — about 35° C (95° F) and no hotter, and carry it with you into the garden.

3) Using a sharp pair of pruners, cut off the selected stem just above a leaf stalk. Be sure to remove no more stem than is absolutely necessary. Immediately put the cut stem into the bucket of warm water. (This is very important, as air must be prevented from entering the cut end; if it does, an air lock occurs and the

stem is unable to take up any of the water; this will shorten the life of your cut roses.) Stems can be immersed almost up to the neck of the blooms. Be careful not to splash water on the petals as this can mark them. Place the blooms as you cut them around the rim of the bucket.

4) Bring the bucket into the house and re-cut each stem **under warm water**, about 1 cm ($^1/_2$″) from the end. The cut should be slanted so the maximum surface area is exposed to the water. (The reason for re-cutting roses under water is to ensure there are no air blockages in the end of the stem.) Leave the roses in the warm water until it cools.

5) Now the blooms are ready to be conditioned (hardened). Take the roses out of the bucket and remove any leaves and thorns that will be below the water level in the vase. (Foliage under water will start to decay very quickly and the resulting bacteria will shorten the life of your cut flowers

Next, fill up a bucket with fresh, cool water and add a floral preservative. Put the roses back into the bucket and again re-cut the stems under water. Set the container in a cool, dark place for about four hours. The ideal temperature for conditioning roses is around 2–5° C (36–41° F).

The roses are now ready for arranging.

Wilted roses

Roses that have prematurely wilted can be freshened up as follows: first, straighten the necks and stems, then completely immerse in a large container of 38° C (100° F) water. Cut off about 2.5 cm (1″) of the old stem and leave in the water for an hour or two. You should now be able to enjoy the blooms for a little while longer. (A rose stem will assume the shape it is in when it absorbs water — if you don't straighten the bent neck and stem, the rose will stay that way.)

Pruning

U NDERSTANDING THE REASON FOR PRUNING takes the mystery out of this very important gardening operation and makes it easier for you to prune effectively.
Basically there are three main reasons why a rose should be pruned:

1) The natural growth habit of a rose bush is to send up shoots from the base, but, because they are not of a permanent nature, in a few years when shoots deteriorate, the plant channels its energy into new growth. Left to itself, the old, worn-out wood becomes less productive, resulting in small, poor-qual-

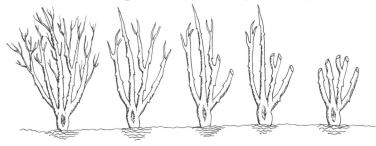

ity flowers. Pruning limits and removes these unproductive canes, thereby allowing the plant's energy to be directed toward producing vigorous growth with better flowers. Pruning also restricts the number of shoots so the root system is not unduly taxed; this is especially important with newly-planted roses.

2) To remove dead, diseased or damaged wood. Also thin and twiggy canes that will produce few, if any, flowers. Pruning is also done to open up the centre of the bushes when growth becomes congested.

3) To shape and trim the bushes.

Like most gardening operations, pruning roses is not an exact science. Many rose growers, while following the basic principles, have developed their own special pruning techniques to suit the location they live in and the varieties they grow. So understanding the reasons why you prune will make the whole operation much easier. And one final thought: your roses will probably survive and bloom — even with a terrible pruning job, or none at all.

When to prune

Late winter to early spring

This is the time for pruning all of the Modern roses. Depending on your climate, pruning should begin **just before the bushes break dormancy**. (In cold prairie provinces and states this could be mid-April to early May.)

Mid-summer to early fall

Generally, the only roses pruned at this time are the Rambler and the non-recurrent (once-flowering) Old Garden roses. These are all pruned after flowering; the subsequent growth they make after pruning will bear next year's flowers. (Unlike Hybrid Teas that flower on wood produced the same year.) Summer pruning should usually be fairly gentle.

Late fall to early winter

Some rosarians swear by pruning at this time; others say to never prune a rose at this time. However, a balanced approach is recommended: prune any badly diseased or infested canes; Climbers can be lightly pruned now, and Modern roses can have their canes shortened prior to being mounded for the winter. The main pruning should be left to early spring.

Pruning equipment

You will need the following:

- A **sharp** pair of pruners (secateurs).

- Long-handled (at least 45 cm/18″) lopping shears for extra thick canes, or hard-to-reach places. (A pruning saw can be used for really thick wood, but lopping shears are easier to use.)

- A heavy pair of leather gardening gloves. (Try to get the ones that extend up the arm a little.)

Pruners

The best type of pruners are ones with scissor-like action. Those with only one cutting edge that presses down on a flat "anvil" can crush the stems — especially if the cutting blade is not very sharp.

How to prune

When cutting a rose cane there is a right way and a wrong way of doing it. Cuts should be made in such a manner that the incidence of die-back is kept to a minimum. Any dead wood on a rose cane becomes a potential lurking place for pests and diseases.

Pruning cuts should be made 1 cm ($^1/_2$″) above a bud eye, cutting at a 45° angle, sloping away and downwards from the bud as shown in the illustration on p. 36.

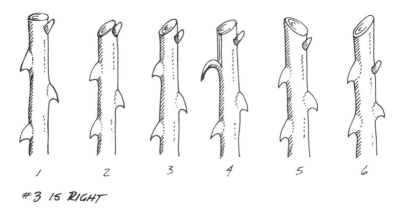

1 *2* *3* *4* *5* *6*

#3 IS RIGHT

The shoot (which grows from the bud eye) will develop in the direction the bud is pointing; when making the cut, therefore, select the bud that will provide the growth in the direction you want. (Sometimes bud eyes further down the cane will produce more vigorous shoots than the top ones.)

Identifying buds

A bud or "bud eye" is in actual fact a condensed shoot that contains the embryo leaves and flowers. On a rose cane these buds are found immediately above the point where the old leaf stalk joined the stem: these are known as leaf-axil or axillary buds. At pruning time most of these buds are easily identifiable as little half-circle bulges on the stems. On older canes sometimes the buds are quite imperceptible; if this is the case, look for the horizontal scar where the old leaf was and assume that a bud will develop from just above it. Later on, if it turns out there was no bud there after all, then not to worry; the cane can be pruned back to a lower bud or shoot.

Remember, buds are not always where you would like them to be. If this is the case, you can do one of two things: cut the canes at the height you want, and later remove any dead ends; or cut to a lower, visible bud.

Roses, like other plants, have latent or dormant buds (you can barely see them) that are only stimulated into growth if an actively growing shoot is removed, either accidentally or deliberately. This explains the sudden appearance of a bud — seemingly from nowhere. (These latent buds are found on either side of a primary bud: see "Thumb Pruning," p. 38.)

Pruning in cold-winter areas

This is probably the easiest — though often most heartbreaking — of all pruning. In sub-zero climates very few canes survive above the protective mound, so pruning mostly consists of removing the winter-killed canes and cutting back to sound, outward-growing buds. Twiggy canes, any shoots that are soft, sappy and blackened at the top, or any that cross and rub against another cane, should all be pruned out.

> When pruning hybrid Rugosas, don't be too hasty to remove what appears to be frost-damaged wood. Oftentimes, healthy, green shoots will appear on a cane you were sure was dead.

Frost-damaged canes are usually light brown or black in appearance, with no green or reddish-brown hue to them. When cut, the inner pith is brown. Frost damage begins at the top of the cane and runs progressively down the stem — sometimes the wood is killed right to the base.

> The Species and some of the Shrub roses that are very winter-hardy with minimum winter-kill are best left to their natural growth habits, with pruning kept to a minimum as you can very easily spoil the shape of these roses just by removing a wrong cane.

Starting from the top, work down the cane until you encounter healthy wood — the pith should be white or slightly greenish. (Keep in mind that as rose wood ages the pith is not so white; be careful you don't mistake older cane wood for frost damage.)

If there is doubt about a suspect cane, leave it — as quite often a cane you thought to be dead is not so dead after all. One sure indication of frost-damaged wood is it has a lighter feel to it. (Of course, you only find this out *after* the cane has been cut, but it is still very useful to know because as you start approaching healthy wood, the weight changes.) Remember, the correct way to remove winter-kill is *little by little* — this prevents the accidental removal of sound wood.

Thumb pruning

No matter how judicious the pruning, invariably more buds will start to develop than is desirable. These should be removed to prevent a mass of blind shoots (ones that don't bloom) and crossing laterals marring the bush. Thumb pruning (pinching out) greatly affects the eventual shape of the bush as it controls the number of buds that are allowed to develop. Excess shoots should be pinched out while still small — less than 2.5 cm (1"). This is done in the spring after the main pruning, once the shoots are growing, and you know what you've got.

Try to encourage bud eyes to develop in the middle of the canes as this is where the best shoots are located. For the production of specimen blooms on large-flowered varieties, thumb pruning is essential.

Latent buds that are triggered into growth (sometimes the damaged, primary shoot will continue to grow if it has not been completely knocked off) should be thumb pruned if you don't need them.

Winter Protection

I N AREAS WHERE THE TEMPERATURE does not normally drop below -9° C (16° F), winter protection should not be necessary — except for the very tender Tea roses (but it's doubtful many people grow these). Below -12° C (10° F), some form of protection is necessary for most roses. In extremely cold areas that experience minimum temperatures of -23° C (-10° F) and lower, only the hardiest of Shrub and Species roses will survive without some form of protection. Hybrid Teas and Floribundas will all require heavy protection.

Preparing roses for winter

As the correct depth at which to plant the bud union plays such a vital part in winter survival, the time to start preparing roses for winter begins at planting time.

Throughout the growing season, keep plants healthy by maintaining good cultural practices. Roses that are healthy going into winter survive much better than bushes that have been growing under stress during the summer.

Another factor that plays an important part in helping roses survive the winter is the proper hardening-off of the canes. Growth that is soft and sappy will experience severe winter-kill when the heavy fall frosts arrive. To help plants slow down and get ready for winter, the following is recommended:

1) Reduce the amount of watering (and application of fertilizer if that's what you have been doing). If fall weather is extremely dry, the bushes must receive *some* water, but not as much as during the height of the growing season. Just before the bushes are mounded up, give them a final soaking; the soil should not be dry over the winter months.

2) Towards the end of summer, leave the spent blooms on the plants: allowing hips to develop gives the plant the idea that the growing season is over for another year, and it's time to get ready for winter. It's particularly important to do this with repeat bloomers such as Hybrid Teas, as their natural growth habit is to keep making new shoots and blooms until brought to a sudden halt by killing frosts. By not cutting off the old blooms you somewhat assist these types of roses to slow down the production of soft, new shoots. (Many of the Modern roses do not set hips, so just leave on the dead blooms.)

In years when the weather cooperates and the bushes are gradually inured to colder conditions, there is far less winter-kill than if plants are suddenly plunged into a deep freeze.

Mounding up the bushes

Before the actual mounding of bushes, the following tasks should be done:

- Clean up around bushes, picking up dead leaves: these can invite the development of fungal diseases under the mound.

- Remove all broken canes and suckers and any new sappy shoots.

- Give your roses a final soaking, providing the soil is not already moist enough. This final watering should be done several days before the ground freezes up.

- Cut the tops of the canes down to about 45–50 cm (18–20″) high.

- Make sure that you have the covering material handy.

Covering materials

Materials used should be light, fluffy, and have good insulating properties, for example:

- Dry, well-pulverized soil.

- Dry sawdust (redwood sawdust is excellent).

- Dry peat moss.

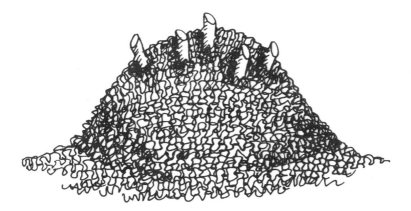

- Dry straw (should only be used as an **additional** covering for the top part of the canes).

- Snow (a natural insulator that gives **additional** protection to already mounded roses).

Fresh leaves are not recommended as they tend to mat and form a soggy mound that will hold moisture and hence rot the canes. The ideal is to keep the canes quite dry.

Being guided by the weather, mound roses before the soil freezes solid for winter. No harm will come to the bushes if they are mounded up a little earlier (many rosarians mound their roses a few weeks before freeze-up, with excellent results), but if sudden sub-zero temperatures arrive and the plants have not been covered, much damage can result, so better to be safe than sorry.

If soil is to be used, it should be brought from another part of the garden and not scraped up from around the bushes.

Heap the covering material over the canes to a height of **at least 30 cm (12″)** If practical, the mound can be even higher, as the more that is covered, the more live wood there will be come spring.

Gently shake bushes as you cover them to ensure material runs down around each cane. If the material settles before it freezes, then more should be added to maintain the height.

Be sure that the mound is not only high enough but wide enough for adequate protection. Evergreen boughs or straw can be placed over the mound for added insulation; this covering will also prevent the wind from blowing away any of the covering material.

Before mounding the bushes, remove any remaining leaves. This is a precaution against possible damage from mildew, botrytis, or other fungus diseases that can start when foliage is covered.

When using dry peat moss as your covering material, to prevent it from all blowing away, spray it lightly with water so the top forms a thin crust that will freeze.

The purpose of mounding roses is to protect them from the elements: the main enemies being cold, drying winds, winter sun and temperature fluctuations. A winter hazard to all plants is the repeated freezing and thawing action that breaks roots, splits canes and crowns, and can even heave plants out of the ground. So the mound not only insulates the canes, but ensures that the soil remains frozen until spring. In areas that experience chinooks (periodic, warm, west winds), increase the amount of insulating material on top of the mound so the soil stays frozen.

Mounding the canes as outlined above will protect tender roses even in areas where the mercury dips to -40° C or F. (In many ways, it's easier to protect roses in areas where temperatures stay below freezing all winter than in more temperate zones that experience drastic fluctuations of temperature, particularly in late winter.)

Beware of raised beds, especially those with brick or stone walls. In such beds, plants should be at least 46 cm (18″) from the edges, as cold will penetrate sideways into the beds.

If you have roses that were not planted at the correct depth originally, they can either be dug up and buried in the same way as container plants, or mounded higher than normal. Replant at the correct depth next spring.

Roses in containers

Even in mild-winter areas, container plants will need some form of protection during cold spells. Roses, along with most other plants, do not like it when the soil inside the container freezes solid. To prevent this, containers can be banked-up with insulating material or placed in an unheated shed or garage — again covering the pots for additional protection. Roses should never be stored for the winter inside a warm, dry house.

In cold-winter areas the best form of protection is to completely bury the plants in the ground. This can be done in two ways:

1) Prune the tops so the canes are of a more manageable length. Give the plant a good soaking. Dig a trench and bury the container horizontally. (Roses are best buried on their side; if buried upright, water can lie on the crowns when the ground thaws in spring, rotting them.)

   Place a couple of bamboo canes to mark the exact location of the plant, then cover with well-pulverized soil that is on the dry side. The sides of the container should be covered with at least 15 cm (6″) of soil. This ensures that the bud union — in the centre of the container — will be adequately protected. An additional covering of straw and evergreen boughs can be placed on top of the soil for increased protection. Carefully dig up the plants in the spring.

2) Prune the tops of the canes and remove the plants from the containers. Shake the soil off the roots and soak the bushes in a garbage can full of water. Dig a trench that is large enough to accommodate the plants lying horizontally. Bundle the bushes together and tie with rope; lie them on their side in the trench. Make sure the canes are covered with at least 15 cm (6″) of fine soil: **do not cover with wet and lumpy soil.**

   Above ground, mound up with another 15 cm (6″) of soil, again making sure the bud unions are covered with a good 30 cm (12″) of soil. Evergreen boughs or straw can be placed on top for added protection. The bundles are uncovered in the spring (pull them up carefully by the rope), and the plants are treated as bare-root bushes.

Physiological drought

The combination of sun, drying winds, and frozen or partly frozen ground can be very deadly not just to roses but to all plants. Under these conditions the phenomenon of physiological drought can occur: there is sufficient water in the soil, but as the ground is frozen, this moisture is unavailable to the plant. The drying winds and sun speed up transpiration (the process by which plants lose water in the form of water vapour into the atmosphere), however, the roots are unable to extract enough water to compensate for this, resulting in the dehydration of plant tissue, with buds and canes shrivelling up. In severe cases the whole plant will die. Strong, drying winds in the spring that cause plants to lose water vapour faster than it is replaced can also be responsible for physiological drought — even when the soil is not frozen.

This is an excellent method of protecting roses over the winter, and one I strongly recommend. I have had the experience of roses being buried like this for one-and-one-half years; when they were finally dug up (I had forgotten where I buried them), the canes were a healthy green and the bud eyes were nice and plump.

Do not bury roses where snowmelt lies in the spring, or in badly drained ground.

Tree roses must be dug up and buried in the same way as container roses; Climbers and Rambler roses must have their lengthy canes taken down from the supports and similarly buried. Not an easy procedure, I'll admit, but there are some rosarians who successfully manage it.

Removing the protective covering

Do not remove the protective covering too soon. Many plants that actually make it through the winter are killed because they are uncovered prematurely — they become victims of springkill.

Some dos and don'ts

- **Don't** uncover the plants too early. An indication that it is safe to remove the protective mound is when you notice the buds on the native Trees starting to break into leaf.

- **Do** remove the covering gradually, not all at once; this is insurance against losing the whole plant to a cold snap that might follow.

- New buds and shoots are very susceptible to low temperatures, so **do** keep straw, burlap or peat moss handy to cover them in the event of a late, heavy, spring frost.

- **Don't** poke and probe around the mound looking for signs of life; you can easily damage developing buds and shoots. With gardening it's good to remember that *patience is a virtue.*

- **Don't** ever uncover roses in the open ground if the soil is still frozen.

- **Do** make sure that the soil in containers is *completely thawed* before exposing the plants to the elements. If the soil is frozen in the pots when you dig them up, put the containers in an unheated shed or garage to *slowly* thaw out. Once the soil is able to absorb moisture, give the pots a light watering: this can prevent possible desiccation of the bushes. Only when the soil is completely thawed should the containers be put outside and watered more heavily.

Why your roses never made it

- Poor quality plant to begin with.

- Bud union not planted deep enough.

- Plant in poor condition going into winter (came under stress during the growing season).

- Plant not protected, or protective mound applied *after* very severe frosts.

- Covering material too heavy, too wet or having bad insulating properties.

- Protective mound not high enough or wide enough.

- Soil too dry going into winter.

- Protection removed too early.

- Roses planted in a bad location: snowmelt area; too close to the sides of raised beds. (Frost penetrates horizontally quite a distance, especially if the wall is stone or cement.)

Finally, don't be too quick to discard what might appear to be a dead plant. Even if all the canes are dead above ground, the bush will still send up new basal shoots providing the bud union was adequately protected.

Keeping Your Roses Healthy

The secret — proper care and attention

THE BEST WAY TO AVOID many problems is to properly care for your roses during the growing season. It's no coincidence that healthy, vigorous plants are much less vulnerable to pests and diseases than roses that have been badly grown and neglected.

To start with, only buy top quality plants. It's much easier to maintain healthy roses if they were that way to start with.

Roses should always be grown in situations that suit them. For example, roses that are grown in shade will have continual problems with powdery mildew — you will always be fighting a losing battle.

Watch your roses! The alert gardener pays close attention to the plants; this way problems with pests and diseases can often be minimized before they reach epidemic proportions. Being observant will also help identify any plants that are under stress from lack of water, too much water, or generally poor growing conditions. Remember the old adage: "A stitch in time ..."

Every gardener should own, and use, a magnifying glass; it's indispensable in helping to diagnose plant problems. For instance, what at first appeared to be dust on the underside of leaves, when examined under a magnifying glass, turns out to be not dust, but spider mites.

Not all insects are pests

A garden without insects would be a silent, sterile place. There would be no flowers, no Trees, no birds, no bees, no plants — nothing.

We need the insects. They pollinate our plants, they contribute to soil aeration and fertility, they help clean up our garbage, they control weeds and they feed everything: fish, birds, mammals, reptiles, amphibians and even us. Yes, without insects this would be a sorry world indeed.

Considering the vast number of different insects, very few can be classed as garden pests. Indeed, many of them can be termed **beneficial insects** as they help keep the real villains under control.

Beneficial insects can be divided into two general groups: predators and parasites. The predacious insects are those that hunt and kill their prey by devouring them on capture. Parasitic insects, on the other hand, live on other insects, keeping them alive for a time to supply food. Parasites usually lay their eggs on or within the host insect. The hatching larvae gorge on their host, causing its eventual demise.

We must remember that the greatest enemies of insect life are other predatory and parasitic insects. The plant-eating insects are kept in check by their insect-eating counterparts. So instead of indiscriminately killing every insect we see on our plants, we should learn to recognize the beneficial ones. Some of our insect allies include **ground beetles, hoverflies, lacewings, ladybugs, parasitic wasps and tachnid flies**. A good field guide can help identify these beneficials.

Rose pests

Insect populations can appear quite suddenly, especially in the spring, or during hot weather. If you experienced a heavy infestation one year, be on the lookout for similar problems the following year.

Aᴘʜɪᴅs: Small (adults roughly 2 mm ($^1/_{10}$") soft-bodied, usually pear-shaped insects, either green, pink or brown in colour.

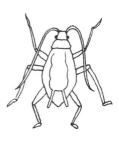

They feed in colonies on young shoots, buds and leaves. They appear in early spring and can be troublesome throughout the season.

Symptoms: Shoots and buds stunted and deformed. Young leaves become twisted, yellowed, puckered and distorted. Aphids excrete honeydew making plant surfaces sticky; ants come after the honeydew.

Control: A forceful jet of water to knock them off will often do the trick. Alternatively, spray with insecticidal soap.

Cᴀᴛᴇʀᴘɪʟʟᴀʀs, ɢᴇɴᴇʀᴀʟ: Destructive larvae of moths and butterflies. Loopers, leaf-rollers, woolybears, brown tails and tent caterpillars are just a few of the villains. Caterpillars come in a variety of sizes and colours. Names often correspond to their appearance, their host or their antics. Generally, caterpillars feed at night and try to avoid detection during the day. Most are active during spring to mid-summer.

Symptoms: Leaves with large, irregular holes that are sometimes stripped to the midrib. Webs or "tents" protecting large colonies of caterpillars. Leaves rolled up or stuck together protecting individual caterpillars. Flower buds eaten, or leaves pulled together with silken threads. Dark pellets of excrement on the leaves.

Control: Hand-pick and destroy. Curled-up leaves can be pried apart and the culprits exposed. Cut out and destroy the large communal tents. To reduce hiding places for cocoons, keep garden free of litter, old pots and lumber (Some of the hairy caterpillars may cause skin irritations, so wear gloves.)

LEAFHOPPERS: Small, slender, wedge-shaped insects, pale-yellow to pale-green in colour. Leafhoppers jump and fly off when disturbed. They feed on the undersides of leaves.

Symptoms: Light, pinpoint mottling and stippling of upper leaf surfaces. In severe attacks the leaves are peppered with tiny, yellowish-white specks, and damaged leaves fall prematurely. The stippled effect is caused by the leafhoppers sucking out the green chlorophyll from the leaves. The pale, mottled skins stuck to the undersides of leaves are a useful indication that leafhoppers are responsible for the damage.

Control: Keep plants well-watered. Roses grown close to walls, in shade, or where the soil is always dry are more susceptible to attack. Eliminate weeds and clean up all garden litter regularly to reduce hiding places for the overwintering eggs. Leafhoppers are vectors of virus disease.

LEAF-ROLLING SAWFLY: Small, shiny, black flies, somewhat resembling flying ants. Related to bees and wasps, these insects do mainly cosmetic damage to roses.

Symptoms: Leaves have edges rolled down and inwards lengthwise towards the midrib. Rolled leaves resemble cylinders. Symptoms usually appear quite suddenly.

Control: Hand pick and destroy infested leaves. Some cultivars, such as "Peace" and "Queen Elizabeth," seem more prone to attack. Cultivate soil around the bushes in the fall to help reduce overwintering numbers.

ROSE CURCULIO (WEEVIL): Sometimes called a snout beetle, this insect is becoming a real pest on the prairie.

Adult weevil is about 8 mm ($^1/_4$") long, hard bodied, with dull, reddish back and long black conspicuous snout (rostrum) with a pair of elbowed antennae (sense organs) toward the tip. Snout tends to curve downward. Eggs laid in flower buds hatch into small, white, legless grubs that fall on the ground

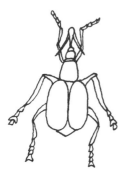

and overwinter in the soil at the base of the bushes.

Symptoms: Buds riddled with fairly neat holes. The sepals on an opening bud are not perforated, just the flower petals in between. Holes are drilled vertically, thus creating a zipper-effect. Perforated buds wilt, turn a dry brown and fail to open; or buds that do manage to open have petals with holes and brown edges throughout. The slow-moving weevils curl up and drop to the ground when disturbed. This pest is particularly fond of the hybrid Rugosas, and can appear in May just as the first buds form.

Control: Carefully (without alerting them to your presence) knock the weevils into a small container, and destroy them. Remove damaged flower buds to prevent the larvae from hatching, thus reducing their numbers for next year. Always clean up fallen leaves, hops, and blooms around the base of the bushes in the fall.

Rose Gall Wasp: Small, inconspicuous, wasp-like insect that lays its eggs in rose stems and branches. Growth-inducing chemicals are also injected along with the eggs, causing plant cells in the vicinity of the intrusion to produce abnormal growth in the form of large swellings or galls. The larvae develop within the galls, overwinter in them, then emerge as adults the following spring.

Symptoms: Large, ugly, wart-like swellings about the size of a mandarin orange on the canes. Galls can be either smooth, mossy, or covered with spines. Often found low down on the bushes close to the soil. On cutting open the woody galls you'll find the larvae inside little chambers.

Control: Prune out and destroy infested stems and galls.

Rose Slug Sawfly: Small, dark, slimy, slug-like larvae feed on leaf surfaces before dropping to the soil to pupate. Larvae overwinter in cocoons in the soil.

Symptoms: Upper leaf surfaces eaten, leaving the veins and the

transparent skin of the leaf intact. Damaged portions turn brown and dry, producing a skeletonized, glazed effect. Look for dark, slimy "slugs" on the leaves.
Control: Hand-pick damaged leaves. (Usually damage is spotty, seldom very extensive.)

SPIDER MITES: Tiny pests, barely visible to the naked eye. Related to spiders, this pest feeds by sucking sap from the undersides of leaves. They are wingless, and vary in colour from green to yellow to brick red to black. Spider mites reproduce rapidly, especially during hot weather.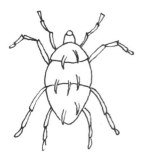
Symptoms: Initially, leaves appear paler in colour with tiny yellowish specks. As infestations develop, foliage becomes mottled, bronzy, dried-out looking, eventually curls up and drops off. Leaves closest to the ground are usually the first invaded. (On first appearances the undersides of the leaves might look as though they are covered with dust splashed up by the rain, however, a closer inspection — using a hand lens — will reveal the real culprits. In severe attacks there can be extensive webbing over the plants.
Control: Keep beds clean around the bushes to eliminate hiding places for over-wintering pests. During the growing season, regularly spray the undersides of the leaves (especially those close to the ground) with a strong jet of water to dislodge any pests. A water wand is very useful for this operation. Roses planted too close to walls (dry air), or plants under stress due to water shortage are often attacked.

TARNISHED PLANT BUG (BISHOP BUG, CAPSID OR LYGUS BUG): Sap-sucking insects that feed on leaves, shoots and flower buds. Adults are about 6 mm ($^1/_4$") long, brown in colour with mottled spots of black, white, yellow and reddish brown and a prominent V-shaped, yellowish mark on the back. Nymphs are greenish yellow, slightly smaller, and wingless. A distin-

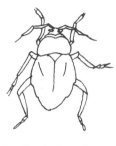

guishing feature of this pest is the flattened, oval to almost square-shaped appearance of the body.

Symptoms: Deformed leaves; brown callouses on leaves and buds; terminal shoots disfigured, stunted and blackened; buds that are malformed, lopsided and fail to open; dead buds; sepals on top of flower buds twisted and puckered; open blooms misshapen and discoloured. Flat-backed bugs found wandering over flower buds. Adults are very evasive and quickly fly away when disturbed.

Control: Not easy to control because of the elusive nature of this pest. Try dusting the foliage and buds with a natural insecticide containing rotenone and diatomaceous earth (fossilized marine plants).

THRIPS (THUNDER FLIES): Very tiny, flying insects that scrape and

injure flower surfaces, then suck up the sap that oozes into the wounds. They mainly feed on the juices from buds and open blooms. In hot, dry weather the pest arrives in hordes.

Symptoms: Petals badly bruised in places, and discoloured with light-brown, translucent blotches or spots — especially around the edges. Deformed flowers, or buds that fail to open. Damage most often occurs to the tighter, fuller buds of large-flowering roses, particularly white, yellow and pink varieties. A close inspection of an opening bloom will probably reveal the insects slithering for cover between the petals.

Control: Again, very difficult. Spunbonded covers made from a fabric-like polyester that allows light, air and moisture to pass through — but not insects — have recently been used to protect blooms from thrips, with good results.

TORTRIX MOTH CATERPILLARS (ROSE MAGGOT, LEAF ROLLERS, LEAF TIERS): The caterpillars of the tortrix moth (there are several species) differ from other caterpillars in that they draw leaves around themselves with silken threads as they feed. The caterpillars are green or brown, with prominent black or brown heads. They are about 6 mm ($^1/_4$″) in length, and they feed on buds and leaves under the cover of darkness.

Symptoms: Leaves rolled up in tubes and drawn together with silk webbing. Caterpillars usually present inside the rolled-up leaves. Tortrix moth caterpillars can be identified by their habit of wriggling backwards when disturbed and bailing out by dropping from the plants on silk threads. These caterpillars also bore neat, round holes in flower buds.

Control: Handpick affected leaves, crushing the caterpillars inside. Remove infested buds.

Pesticides

I have deliberately avoided making any reference to using chemical pesticides. I feel they have no place in the home garden and should not be used. There is ample evidence that once you get on the pesticide treadmill, you will have to keep on spraying to attain results, and, even then, there is no guarantee that the pesticide will even be effective. One thing is certain, however, that once you introduce chemical pesticides into the garden you will kill untold numbers of beneficial insects. And remember this: *kill a beneficial insect and you inherit their work.*

The lens effect

Beware of the lens effect. Even when using innocuous products, damage to foliage can occur when strong sunlight shines through droplets of moisture on the leaves. In effect, the droplets act like a magnifying glass resulting in yellowish spots or rings that appear a day or two after the foliage has been sprayed. To avoid this problem, never spray (or water, for that matter) your roses in full sun.

Non-hazardous controls

Insecticidal soaps are safe alternatives to hazardous chemicals. Made from potassium salts of fatty acids, these are straight soaps, and, unlike detergents and washing-up liquid, contain no chemicals that might damage plants. These are very effective against aphids. When preparing a solution, fill up the sprayer first with water, then add the insecticidal soap. This prevents the soap from foaming.

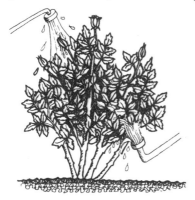

Water — it's a knockout!

A strong jet of water from a garden hose will dislodge many insects, especially aphids. It's a knockout, too, for controlling spider mites, as these pests dislike water. When going after these blighters, concentrate on the undersides of leaves.

Rose diseases

BLACKSPOT: Probably the most common rose disease, and the one most easily identified. Infections can begin in spring and continue through the growing season. Particularly troublesome during periods of warm, wet weather. Spores are spread to nearby bushes by drips, rain splashes, or watering. Spores overwinter chiefly on dormant buds, shoots and canes. *Symptoms:* Dark brown or black spots with irregular fringed edges on leaf surfaces. Spots coalesce (grow together) accompanied by yellowing of tissue next to the spots. Leaves drop off prematurely. Symptoms usually appear first on the more mature lower leaves, then spread throughout the bush. Badly infected bushes can be completely defoliated; this drastically lessens the chances of surviving the winter.
Control: Blackspot-damaged leaves cannot be restored, so prevention is the key. If blackspot is a real problem in your garden, try to keep the foliage dry when watering. (The fungus spores need about six to nine hours in water for them to germinate.) Avoid cultivars or varieties that are prone to blackspot. One notorious source, although a lovely rose, is

"Persian Yellow" (*Rosa foetida persiana*); this rose can spread blackspot to all your other roses. Pick up and destroy infected leaves in the fall.

Plants that are grown under ideal conditions — rich soil, well watered, plenty of room and lots of sun — will seldom be bothered with blackspot. (Expect the odd spot or two in the fall as foliage of plants in general deteriorates at this time.)

POWDERY MILDEW: Very common and widespread fungal disease. Infections can begin in the spring and continue throughout the growing season if conditions are favourable. Unlike blackspot that multiplies rapidly during wet weather, powdery mildew flourishes when cool nights are followed by warm days with low humidity and dry leaf surfaces. That's why powdery mildew is often a problem when fall weather is sunny and dry. (Fall nights are always cool.) The fungus overwinters in canes, dormant buds and fallen leaves.

Symptoms: The very first symptoms — often missed by the untrained eye — appear as slightly undulating edges on the young leaves. Disease becomes much more noticeable as tender leaves, shoots and buds are covered with a greyish, powdery coating. (This powdery coating is actually an enormous number of fungal spores.) Leaf surfaces have slightly raised, blister-like areas covered with the fungus. Badly diseased leaves become puckered, twisted and distorted; buds may fail to open. If left unchecked, the whole plant can quickly become completely covered with the unsightly fungal growth. Beneath the powdery coating leaves may turn a reddish-purple, later to drop off prematurely. Severe infections reduce the overall vigour of plants.

Control: By the time symptoms are visible, the pathogen has already invaded plant tissue, and once powdery mildew is established, all you can do is try to stop it spreading. So again, prevention is the key. Improve air circulation around the bushes by avoiding dry, shady sites and growing the plants too close together. Roses grown against walls are invariably troubled by powdery mildew.

Plants that are under stress from lack of water are also very susceptible. Some cultivars are more resistant to powdery mildew, particularly those with waxy leaves. Many of the older, red Hybrid Teas are very prone to this disease.

CANKER: Cankers that affect roses are all caused by various fungi, the three most common are: stem or common canker, brown canker and band canker. While all three cankers affect the canes in slightly different ways, they all have one thing in common: the canker-causing fungi chiefly invade rose tissue throughout wounds in the bark. Wounds can be inflicted by careless pruning, cultivating, dead heading, insects, frost and hail damage, even broken thorns and leaf scars on canes. Canker fungi overwinter on canes and extend the damaged areas the following spring. Spores are spread to other plants by rain and splashing and dripping water from irrigating.

Symptoms: Most of the following symptoms will be evident, no matter which of the cankers is responsible:

- Small, yellow, reddish or purple spots on canes, often around wounds or cut ends of pruned canes.

- The infected areas are lightest brown, often variegated, with a reddish to purple border.

- Cankered areas gradually spread.

- Tissue within the cankered area is sunken, cracked open or split.

- Cankers girdle the canes, resulting in die-back or feeble growth above the cankered area.

- Tiny, black, dot-like fruiting bodies (spores) develop on the cankered canes.

Stem canker is more common on Hybrid Tea varieties, and brown and band canker often affects the lower part of canes that are mounded over the winter.

Control: It goes without saying, but avoid mechanically injuring the canes. Always prune correctly: use sharp pruning tools and never leave stubs that can become entry points for the fungus. Cut out and destroy cankered stems at least 5 cm (2″) below the point of infection. Pruning tools should be dipped in alcohol after each cut, as a precaution against spreading the disease. Avoid overhead irrigation if the disease is already a problem in the garden. Inspect any plants you buy for the telltale cane lesions or coloured spots; beware of bargains — they may not be bargains at all.

A Few Recipes

G OLDEN RULE: DO NOT USE petals or leaves from bushes that have been sprayed with pesticides. The light-coloured tip at the base of a rose petal is quite bitter; if practical, it should be removed before using the petals in a recipe.

Rose Petal Jam

$^1/_2$ lb.	*garden rose petals*	*225 g*
$^1/_2$ lb.	*clear honey*	*225 g*
1 c.	*water*	*300 mL*
	strained juice of 1 lemon	

There should be no dew on the petals. Wash jars and put in warm oven. Put rose petals, honey, and water into a pan and bring to boil. Simmer gently for about 10 minutes or until rose petals are soft. Strain, reserving liquid; put rose petals into hot jars. Return liquid to pan and add lemon juice. Bring to boil and boil until setting point is reached. Cool slightly. Pour into jars and stir well. Cover with waxed circles and seal. Makes three or four little jars.

A Few Recipes

Rose Water

$^1/_2$ lb.	*fragrant red rose petals*	*225 g*
$^1/_4$ lb.	*sugar*	*125 g*
20 oz.	*water*	*600 mL*

Put rose petals, sugar, and water in a pan and simmer for about 10 minutes or until colour and perfume come out. When cool, strain into a clean bottle and store in refrigerator. Keeps for 10 days.

Sugared Rose Petals

rose petals
2 egg whites
granulated sugar

Put egg whites in a bowl and beat until they begin to stiffen. Using tweezers, dip dry petals individually, first into the egg whites, then the sugar, making sure each petal is completely coated. Shake off excess sugar, making sure each petal is still completely coated. Lay out petals on a cookie sheet lined with waxed paper so they do not touch each other. Put the tray in a warm, airy spot to slowly dry and crisp the petals. When quite dry, store in tin or jar between layers of waxed paper. Use as candy, or as a cake decoration.

Rose Brandy

$^1/_2$ lb.	*fragrant red rose petals*	*225 g*
1 lb.	*sugar*	*450 g*
1 c.	*brandy or vodka*	*250 mL*
20 oz.	*boiling water*	*600 mL*

Pour boiling water over the petals and let steep for a few minutes. Strain through a fine sieve, then add the sugar to the liquid. Heat gently to help dissolve the sugar. Remove from heat, and add the brandy or vodka. Bottle.

A Few Recipes

Rose Petal Ice Cream

1 c.	*whipping cream*	*250 mL*
1 Tbsp.	*sugar*	*15 mL*
2 Tbsps.	*strained lemon juice*	*30 mL*
6 Tbsps.	*rose petal jam (see p. 60)*	*90 mL*

Carefully heat the lemon juice and sugar in a small pan. Stirring constantly, bring to the boil, then boil for a couple of minutes. Leave to cool. Whip the cream lightly, add the rose petal jam and cooled lemon syrup. Spoon into containers, cover and freeze until firm.

Rose Honey

$^1/_4$ lb.	*rose petals*	*125 g*
1 lb.	*honey*	*450 g*

Put rose petals and honey in pan and boil for 10 minutes, stirring constantly. Press and strain through a very fine sieve or cloth. Excellent for sore throats.

Potpourri

Roses should be picked early in the morning when the dew is gone. When flowers are picked fresh, more of the essential oil remains after they are dried — and that means more fragrance. Also pick a few rose leaves and small buds, as well as cornflowers, marigolds and delphiniums to add colour.

Pull the flowers carefully apart (not the small buds) and lay out the petals, leaves and buds flat on paper towels. If you have narrow, slatted wooden drying racks, then so much the better. Dry the flowers in a warm, airy place out of direct sun. Turn daily until the petals and leaves are dry and crisp — just like cornflakes. (This will take a week or two, depending on humidity.)

To 4 cups of dried petals, leaves and small buds, add:

2 oz.	*dried orris root*	*50 g*
	(a fixative that preserves the fragrance)	
1 tsp.	*whole allspice*	*5 mL*
2	*cinnamon sticks broken into several pieces*	2
	a few drops of rose oil	

Put it all in a large plastic container and gently shake to thoroughly mix the ingredients. Store tightly closed for about three weeks to allow the fragrances time to blend and mellow. The potpourri is now ready to put in attractive glass containers with removable lids, pomanders (china pots with perforated lids) or open glass or china bowls. Little sachets can be filled to freshen drawers and closets.

Add These Homeworld Titles to Your Library

Attracting Birds
ISBN 0-919433-87-1   64 pp. $5 \frac{1}{2}'' \times 8 \frac{1}{2}''$ $6.95

Canadian Heritage Breadmaking
ISBN 1-55105-016-1   64 pp. $5 \frac{1}{2}'' \times 8 \frac{1}{2}''$ $6.95

Christmas Survival Guide
ISBN 1-55105-019-6   64 pp. $5 \frac{1}{2}'' \times 8 \frac{1}{2}''$ $6.95

Furniture Refinishing Made Easy
ISBN 1-55105-022-6   64 pp. $5 \frac{1}{2}'' \times 8 \frac{1}{2}''$ $6.95

Herbs for Northern Gardeners
ISBN 0-919433-99-5   64 pp. $5 \frac{1}{2}'' \times 8 \frac{1}{2}''$ $6.95

Jams and Jellies
ISBN 0-919433-90-1   48pp. $5 \frac{1}{2}'' \times 8 \frac{1}{2}''$ $4.95

Northern Balcony Gardening
ISBN 0-919433-98-7   64 pp. $5 \frac{1}{2}'' \times 8 \frac{1}{2}''$ $6.95

Pickles and Preserves
ISBN 0-919433-88-x   48 pp. $5 \frac{1}{2}'' \times 8 \frac{1}{2}''$ $4.95

The Prairie Beekeeper
ISBN 1-55105-032-3   64 pp. $5 \frac{1}{2}'' \times 8 \frac{1}{2}''$ $5.95

Winemaking Made Easy
ISBN 1-55105-030-7   64 pp. $5 \frac{1}{2}'' \times 8 \frac{1}{2}''$ $5.95

Look for these and other Lone Pine books at your local bookstore.
If they're unavailable, order direct from:

Lone Pine Publishing
#206, 10426-81 Avenue
Edmonton, Alberta   T6E 1X5
Phone: (403) 433-9333
Fax: (403) 433-9646
Toll free: 1-800-661-9017

#202A 1110 Seymour Street
Vancouver, B.C. V6B 3N3
Phone: (604) 687-5555
Fax: (604) 687-5575